For Holly J.

Copyright © 1993 by Amanda Wallwork.
All rights reserved. Published by Scholastic Inc.,
730 Broadway, New York, NY 10003, by arrangement with Ragged Bears Ltd.
First published in 1993 by Ragged Bears Ltd.
SCHOLASTIC HARDCOVER® is a registered trademark of Scholastic Inc.

Library of Congress Cataloging-in-Publication Data Available

ISBN 0-590-46769-7

12 11 10 9 8 7 6 5 4 3 2 1   3 4 5 6 7 8/9

Printed in Hong Kong

First Scholastic printing, November 1993

NO DODOS

A Counting Book of Endangered Animals

Amanda Wallwork

SCHOLASTIC INC.
New York

1

one whale

2
two tigers

3
three pandas

4

four elephants

5

five frogs

6
six seals

7
seven parrots

8
eight penguins

9

nine dolphins

10

ten turtles

0
... but no dodos

WHALES

The blue whale is the largest creature on earth – larger than thirty elephants together. Over the years, the whale population has declined because whales have been hunted for their meat and oil. Many kinds of whales are now protected, but some countries continue to allow whale hunting.

TIGERS

The tiger is the largest member of the cat family. It lives in the rain forests of Asia. The destruction of the rain forests threatens the tiger's survival. And so do people who still want tiger skins for clothing and for trophies.

PANDAS

The panda is one of the rarest animals in the world. The bamboo forests of China are the panda's natural habitat. These forests are being cleared for farmland, which deprives the panda of its home as well as its only source of food.

ELEPHANTS

Elephants are the biggest land animals. For years they have been hunted and killed for their ivory tusks, which can be carved into jewelry and ornaments. Because ivory is rare and valuable, some people still kill elephants even though that is now illegal.

FROGS

Different kinds of frogs live all over the world in all kinds of habitats. But their numbers are declining because the places where they live are being taken over by people and contaminated by pollution.

SEALS

Seals are endangered because they are hunted for their fur. But they are also affected by pollution. The unspoiled Pacific beaches where seals rear their young are disappearing due to tourist development and pollution. Seals are also considered pests by some fishermen because they compete for fish and can damage fishing nets.

PARROTS

Parrots live in tropical forests in South America, Africa, Asia, and Australia. These forests are being cut down to make wood products and to clear land for farms. Also, continuing demand for live birds as pets means that thousands of parrots are captured every year. Many die during transportation.

PENGUINS

Even though penguins live hundreds of miles from civilization, in Antarctica and New Zealand, they are threatened by pollution of the seas. Also, fishing has severely reduced the amount of food available for penguins.

DOLPHINS

Dolphins are playful and friendly creatures that have always fascinated people. They are featured in ancient fables and works of art. Dolphins are harmed by ocean pollution. And because they cannot breathe underwater, thousands of dolphins drown every year when they get caught in fishing nets.

TURTLES

Tourist development has damaged many of the beaches where turtles go to lay their eggs. Also, turtles are killed for their meat and beautiful shells. Their eggs are considered a delicacy and are often stolen from their nests.

DODOS

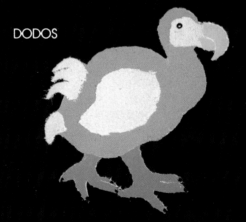

Dodos were birds that couldn't fly. They lived on Mauritius, an island in the Indian Ocean. Years ago people began killing dodos for sport. They were very easy to catch, and soon there were no dodos left at all.

Today the dodo is extinct. There are no more of these birds left on the earth, and there's nothing anyone can do to change that.

But people can help keep other animals from becoming extinct by preserving their natural habitats, cleaning up pollution, and passing laws that protect endangered animals.

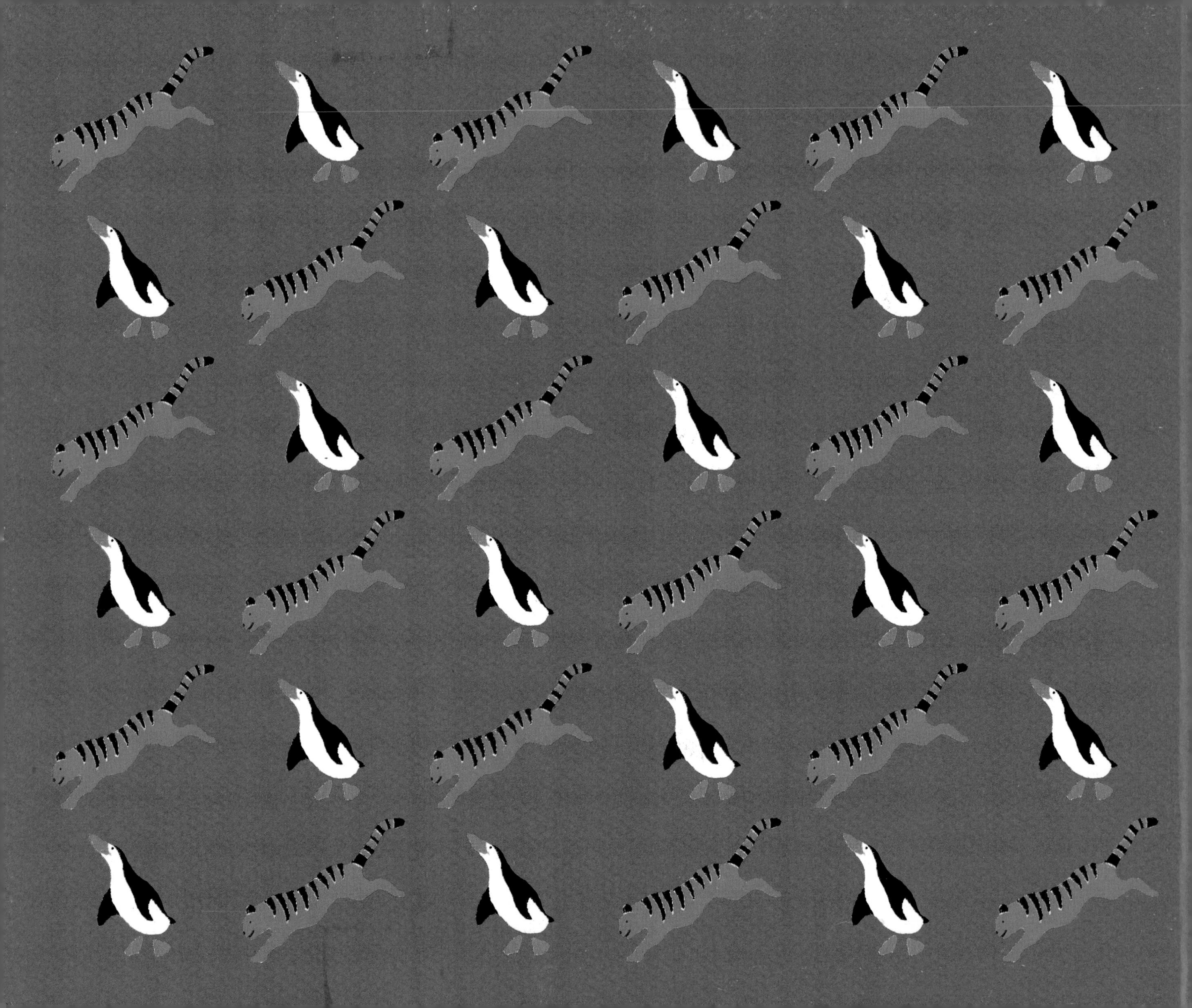